Sebastian...

The Incredible Drawing Dog

THE BARKING CAT

Story and pictures by DAVID MYERS
from the television series devised and written by David Myers

BEAVER BOOKS

For Joy, Jane, Paul,
Adam and Matthew

A Beaver Book
Published by Arrow Books Limited
62-5 Chandos Place, London WC2N 4NW
An imprint of Century Hutchinson Ltd
London Melbourne Sydney Auckland
Johannesburg and agencies throughout the world

First published by André Deutsch 1987
Beaver edition 1987

Text and illustrations © David Myers 1987

Printed and bound in Italy

ISBN 0 09 954120 3

Hello, dear reader,

I do hope you enjoy this rather strange and wonderful story.

I've had great fun doing the pictures – especially the one on page 19. Professor Kibble obviously likes pictures, wouldn't you agree? Just look at the number in his room!

I'll let you into a secret – I HATE drawing bicycles. Look at the one I've drawn on page 8. I'm not very proud of it but I promise to try harder next time.

Meanwhile, I must knuckle down to work on my next book.

See you soon!

Very best wishes,

Hasn't she got a nice Smile?

Mrs Honey was a charming little old lady.

Can you spot a frog in my picture?

She adored animals. She was crazy about them. And of all the animals she loved *cats* best of all. She owned one herself – it was called Blossom.

A magnificent cat, isn't it? Now Blossom was rather different from other cats. Do you know why? Well, Blossom didn't miaow like other cats.

Blossom BARKED!
  Yes, BARKED!! WOOF, WOOF, WOOF, WOOF-WOOF!! That's odd, don't you agree?

Nevertheless, Mrs Honey loved Blossom and wherever she went Blossom went too. "There goes Mrs Honey and her barking cat," the neighbours would chuckle.

But Mrs Honey was too sensible to be upset by their remarks.

Then one day it happened! Mrs Honey got on a bus to go shopping.

As soon as she sat down Blossom started to bark. WOOF-WOOF-WOOF! The conductor was livid. Just look at him.

"Who's brought a dog on my bus?" he raged. "Own up! Own up!! You know it's not allowed."

"It's *not* a dog!" cried Mrs Honey. "It's my cat! My cat, Blossom!"

"A barking cat?" yelled the conductor. "Are you making fun of me, Madam? I'll remind you this is no joking matter!"

Temper!! Temper!!

"I'm not joking," sobbed Mrs Honey. And just then
Blossom gave three loud barks. "WOOF-WOOF-
WOOF!!"

The conductor was staggered. "I can't believe it! I can't
believe it! Now I've seen everything. *Everything*!!"

Oh! Poor Mrs. Honey!

Well, this sort of thing was happening to Mrs Honey so often that she decided to seek the advice of a vet. Here's Blossom at the vet....

"Oh, dear, Oh, dear! There's nothing I can do about this!" said the vet. "Never come across this kind of thing before! *Never*!

"But perhaps a friend of mine can help. He's an ANIMAL IMPERSONATOR. Maybe he can teach Blossom to miaow!"

Mrs Honey took his advice. That very afternoon she went
round to the animal impersonator's home.

"Come in, come in. The vet has just phoned to say you were coming!"

Look at all those pictures on his walls!...

He patted Blossom on the head, led the way inside…

and poured Blossom a huge dish of cream. "I would like you to leave Blossom with me for three and a half days.

"Please leave while he is busy with the cream and
do not worry!"

And here's a sad Mrs Honey leaving the house....

The three and a half days went very slowly for poor
Mrs Honey. She missed Blossom terribly.

And what a lovely sunny day!

When the time came to collect her pet, she was bursting with excitement.

The animal impersonator opened the front door and as
soon as she saw his face she knew all was well. He was
smiling happily....

"Blossom has been a perfect pupil. Purrrrfect!" he laughed. "Come and see for yourself!"

Immediately Mrs Honey entered the room, Blossom leapt
into her arms miaowing and purring, miaowing and purring.

It was a touching and happy moment.

But that's *not* quite the end of the story. You see Blossom
has since become world-famous!

Not for his miaow as you might imagine. But for his PURR!!

The Post Office people were very quick to recognize this
delightful friendly sound.

Blossom now holds one of the most important
Post Office jobs.

If you don't believe me, just pick up the telephone at any time and listen to his happy purring.